Loom

poems by

Mary Romero

Finishing Line Press
Georgetown, Kentucky

Loom

ACKNOWLEDGMENTS

Able Muse: "The Bedroom Built Around a Tree"
Birmingham Poetry Review: "Penelope At Home"
Crux: "Island, Sea"
Forma: "He Knows the Names of Flowers," "The Weaving of Arachne" and
    "Song of the Sirens"
Measure: "Song of Kalypso"
Mezzo Cammin: "Song of Circe" and "Penelope and Echo"
Peacock Journal: "Testament: to My Son Telemachus"
Slant: "The Other Arrows of Eros"

Publisher: Leah Huete de Maines
Editor: Christen Kincaid
Cover Art: Kayb Weidhas Joseph
Author Photo: Joni Romero
Cover Design: Elizabeth Maines McCleavy

Order online: www.finishinglinepress.com
            also available on amazon.com

Author inquiries and mail orders:
Finishing Line Press
P. O. Box 1626
Georgetown, Kentucky 40324
U. S. A.

Table of Contents

BOOK III: RAVELING THE SHROUD

INTERLUDE: IN WHICH SIRENS CRYING BEAUTY WILL LURE YOU WITH YOUR STORY

BOOK IV: BINDING THE SELVAGE

for Ben

"Fervently wish your journey may be long."

~ C. P. Cavafy, "Ithaca"

PROLOGUE: A REQUEST FOR THE READER'S SUSPENSION OF DISBELIEF

Listen—a woman
whose sphere is limited
to a confined island

can still compose an epic
with the fibers
her fingers grasp.

Will you let her tell it?
A tale without a field
of spilled blood,

a speared cyclops,
nymph or purple bed.
Instead—a son

to tender into the world,
parched bulbs to wet
beneath the mulch,

and a faithful thread
that finds its eye
even in the wind.

Will you consider it improbable
as taming the sea
with a pair of needles?

A sad net cast
over the frantic foam.

Reader, consider it possible.

Book I:

Lashing the Warp

PENELOPE AT HOME

Each time you leave, an eternity sails by.

Our son bobs up, plump-legged, and plummets forwards,
　　rummaging in every bin of trash, the imp.

Suddenly running, so swiftly he gains Olympian legs,
　　each morning vaulting out of bed, hungry—always

hungry. So many meals to mark the frenzy of days.
　　And while he rises, I forget myself. My hair grays.

What must it be like to leave? To stand
　　amongst the unaging seas and remain?

And when you return, a salt-washed figurehead,
　　what to say? What to say when you ask,

"What have you done while I was away?"

FRAGMENT: [MY SON CLINGS]

my son clings   fading skirt

screams   an inch of door

between us   blue ice

shivering

        I fear

I have welcomed these phantoms

because I too fear

what comes in the

        what doesn't

your voice

an eternity of shut doors

THE HOME FRONT

My mind travels so often to you
        that I struggle to rest—

then, when I am present
        as a lizard sunning on a stone—

the thought of you
        startles me like any predator.

We remain at war. Messages return
        with pierced guts soiling the edges

of our sleep. How can we sleep
        when a scythe is hacking at the world?

And to think—yesterday
        I almost mastered a day

without weeping. Was it wrong
        to inhabit such a small, still pool?

Wars have risen here as well
        within my bones—a flame—

the startled animal
        of my son's face, my hand

raised as if to strike, then—
        spilling around his thin body—

here—please—let it ripple
        like the softest song

that never becomes visible—

ITHACA

On islands, all must be made or helped into making:
all babies, birthing goats and sheep and mares,
their slippery offspring licked into the fields.

A dimpled mother harvests wheat, one child on her hip,
her eldest hiding in the grasses, a third
who sways like grain in the sling of her womb. We make

our songs to mimic loons, to whistle haunts,
to become a long arm pulling in the dawn.
The puzzling night, we fill with fire and sound:

slick reeds woven in threes to blow—and bleat
with the riot of sheep—and guts of sheep
to stretch into strings and strum over drumheads,

calloused feet that stamp the pearled grapes flat;
slim cups to slam the nectar down our throats.
And cypress, stripped of bark, then split and smoothed

into swift, yet sinkable ships that carry you
away to war. To take what you have not made.
Or unmake everything of others. Engaged

by Agamemnon, who will always rage for war.
We rage to feed each other; warring to be made.

HE KNOWS THE NAMES OF FLOWERS

With the men shipped off with their spears,
       my son works with the women

at their tending. He knows the leaven
       rising in the rye, and how

to beat it back, and let it rise again.
       He knows the scent of lye,

how fingers blister and wrinkle,
       plunged in steaming tubs,

how linen fibers go firm when wet
       and silk proves delicate. He knows

the river of women's chatter
       coursing alongside every task

and how to shorten such a task
       by singing, or noticing a trio of notes

tumbled from a nearby tree, to mimic
       and call the feathered shyness back.

He sings the names of flowers,
       knows their power lies not in flight,

sinew, or bite, but in the quiet
       confidence that they will return.

TO FAR-EYED ODYSSEUS

To persevere without tasting
       your lips, keen limbs,
       green cluster of laughs—

brings to mind when you'd cajole me, lute in hand,
       stringing out such thrilling yarns
       to excuse another absence.

For you, to whom I'm bound, are boundless
       as I myself, spinning in stillness,
       waiting for you to cease

your endless orbit around what could be.
       Ourselves: separate,
       unsayable stars

that never converge.
       Is our only hope
       for both of us to fall?

ANEMONE AND ASPHODELUS

[Poppy and White Asphodel]

Some would say—my son reminds me—
  that we are plucking souls from the ground

in this act of gathering.
  The scarlet poppies bleeding out

the slain muscles of men;
  each blanched asphodel,

a pale soul left to rise again.
  As though their slender meaning

could only come from being
  one of us. Before they succumb

so quickly to my touch,
  they've offered their fluted bodies

to countless, winged beings all alone.
  How could we imagine

the body and soul of a flower
  is any but its own—

TO NOT WAIVER FROM THE EMPTINESS

Some of it sticks.

I am bathing my son near the sea—a clean rinse
from bronze buckets we warm by the fire.
The stream from it snags the fading light
and sings, sliding over his filthy, flawless skin.
I tousle his hair, and he streaks naked from me,
running down the dunes, and whooping,
back into the sea. Sand-caked and grinning.

He'll need bathing again. And always.

As the clothes will need washing; the spent lilies—
bent as aged backs—will need dead-heading;
the bedsheets: to be soaked, hung dry, pulled taut—
again and again.

       Tossing towel and sandals aside;
adjusting soles into the warm give of sand,
and laughing, I race down to the tide with him.

I am a sieve.
      I am being filled and filled.

Interlude:

In Which the Beguiling Witch Explains Her Situation

SONG OF CIRCE

They call me witch—and worse—not knowing what I do.
It isn't magic, merely a trick of revelation,
a teasing of the veil, a flair for seeing truth.
Not endless damnation—it's only for a short duration,

this... *porcine* transformation. All those men were tested
and proved to act like swine, as many do. Not all.
I simply peeled the mask away, and they attested
to their own demise. When a woman's on top, the thrall

of jealousy will spawn a man's pigheadedness.
The smaller the man, the smaller he needs his women to seem.
A tired song. But oh, the difference with Odysseus:
undaunted poise facing my power... it was a dream.

He loved his wife. But on this isle with pigs by the dozen,
can I be blamed for wanting the only man who wasn't?

Book II:

A Thin Flame Runs Along Her Thread

FRAGMENT: [MONSTERS AND MAD WOMEN]

I hear stories of monsters and mad women
with witchlike ways to summon wanting

Those sailors   the only ones

ever to be tempted   the way they warble

voices haunt us   home

more insidious   bodiless

purple pleasures   evaporate

quartz   contentment

ANNOYED WITH DESIRE

That unraveling snake
        whistling in and out

of every improbable crack
        in one's house.

It will come and go
        when and where it wants—

and it always wants
        for you to chase it.

Is fidelity merely
        an absence of lust?

Is it lust, to hunger
        for another's mind?

I keep watching
        the silky thing,

small spark
        of a conflagration—

as it begins to slip
        under the door—

CAUGHT

To me he seems a supple linden,
       this man leaning across the table,

our repartee: a meal
       scented by smoke

from the lit hearth.
       My words stick.

Thunder shudders my eardrums
       when he speaks, soft and laughing,

and that old, doped arrow nicks,
       loosening limbs.

Lips clam up, a pearl
       of longing on my tongue,

desire painting every pore
       when his gaze follows

the rabbit pace
       of my animal pulse—exposed—

holding my ground
       like a willow in a gale—

I disarmed long ago.
       How could I know

this breathless part of me
       could still breathe—

FRAGMENT: [TO EROS]

You lash us like prisoners

our knees buckle

Every longing, a new whip

        within the

no sound as luscious

              fig-tongued

lips of dahlia

          light rain laces a face

for he thought

sweet   to succumb

Paris in the silver bed

Helen—

he was never worth a war

a blind

AS SHE RAVELS

A shadow looms in the stone arch
        not far from where I weave,

as though you flinch to desecrate
        the sanctuary of my spinning.

I would not have you near—I itch for some repreive
        from gauge, hitch, weave:

the work that is myself—the self I long
        to set aside. You stall, inch near the webbing,

offer to spin a yarn for me: a flaxen tale that lengthens
        with a twist—fleeced mortal, fated unwinding.

Eventually you quiet like a muffled string,
        and beg a fable of me. So I sing:

THE WEAVING OF ARACHNE

The spindle-fingered spinster called Arachne
adored her loom and wove with delicacy;
precision equal to anything a god
could make: a dahlia, a goldenrod.
Her tapestries could breathe, redolent
like perfumed hair, a crush of moss, a scent
escaping from the threads. To see her tide
in lapis-layered yarn was to reside
within it, feel it fringed with foam and hear
its susurration and its song. A deer
could leap out of her rippled field. She'd weave
a spell that only mortals, driven by need,
have learned to cast. The never-discontent
divinities still lack this element
in art: the urgency to breathe another air,
to make, with wrinkling hands, a world elsewhere
that might outlive its source. We've all to gain,
to glean a bitter beauty from our pain.

Enraged, Athena protested, and in a contest
bested her—of course, an unfair test—
how could it ever have been fair?
Exiled, dark-eyed Arachne felt the snare
entrap her. She plaited strings into a noose
around her neck. They hung like roots
beneath a tree, and when she fell, they laced
themselves into a web around her, encased
her purpled body as it split into
a spider's legs and spinnerets, the tissue
of her skin now hard and haired, her abdomen,
once thin, now heavy with silk to spin.
And spin she must to live, as live she must
to spin.

　　　　Listen. Our work cannot be rushed.
It's earned our time as more than future dust—
it lives. And might entangle—or deliver us.

I HEAR WHAT THEY SAY ABOUT ME

Pursued by a hundred and eight; rejected all,
       loved none.

Or bedded each and birthed
       a monstrous god.

One would think these tales
       could never coexist,

yet here they breed
       on opposition.

What if truth was somewhere between
       maidenhair and belladonna?

Here, where sea daffodils
       break the crust of dunes

will you let me be
       a bulb in spring

escaping the ground
       but waiting to open—

HELLEBORE

[Lenten Rose]

Late winter rose,
        you open me
with your petals

of the palest jade:
        shivering in bunches
bent in genuflection.

Oracles of the frigid rain,
        you portend the deepening
of green again.

THE OTHER ARROWS OF EROS

1.   A woman can fall in love twenty times a day.
        Beautiful things, of course, not so much
        Cats as their velvety kittens,
        Delicate leaves in winter,
        Everything that glistens, even the tracks of snails,
        Fossils of imprinted fern once
        Green—green wherever,
        However lit,
        Is longing in a color—
        Jelly's sensuous wobble,
        Kindling curled into sparks, clean
        Linens filled with a lake of wind,
        Movement in trees that is
        Nearly conscious,
        Opal's iridescence, and the surprising
        Purple of eggplant peeking so
        Quaintly among the parsley
        Ruffled by a light rain,
        Smooth skin of a forearm
        Tattooed and itching
        To be touched—anyone
        Undressed is laughable enough to love—
        Volumes and volumes, when someone
        Whistles unconsciously—or writing
        X—two lines
        Yoked together with ink,
        Zest of anything citrus.

2.   Zealous women love a good list,
        Yearn to chronicle all—like
        X's carved in bark to mark a path.
        Why this need to catalogue,
        Valuing the small, even
        Unmemorable details?
        To teach ourselves to hear—a conch
        Shell pressed to the ear? To see a thread
        Running through our odd,

Quixotic lives? To become
Playful as children again, we
Order sounds and make a world from wind.
Notice the potency of this
Mesmerizing balm when you
Lie waiting: place pleasures together like
Kin—whether blackberry
Jam or an
Impish kiss, a bee
Hive's comb, or
God's brightness, fullness
Filling each small seed.
Eros can lavish us with more than
Easy infatuation. Look—what
Desire is born of the bright
Constellations and dirt-wrought
Blooms that make life
Bearable, and sometimes—
Astonishing.

Interlude:

In Which Kalypso Lounges in a Gown of
Too-Sheer and Supple Silver

SONG OF KALYPSO

No chance your mortal bride can thrill you as I do.
Awe-slapped, your lips hung loose at your first sight of me.
She's dusky, dried-up; I'm all gold, with breasts as smooth
as apples in your mouth, or swimming naked in the sea.

And yet your eyes still howl with longing for her when
you shut your ears to my bewitching melody.
I mystify your limbs and mind again. Again
you wake and want your pitiful Penelope.

You've no idea how long my skin was touched only
by wind; how time proves endless whenever you're alone;
how your flushed body, slick—but tricked—still left me lonely;
and how, these seven years, I've both denied and known:

The only way to keep you is to let you suffer.
The only way to love you is to let you love her.

Book III:

Raveling the Shroud

PENELOPE AND ECHO

The suitors keep insisting it is time   *I'm*
to choose, but I refuse to turn into a lonely   *only*
echo, breathing only borrowed   *owed*
sound, surrounded solely by something   *one thing.*
to mimic.

       By my fingers, this loom comes alive: *I've*
each lilting, familiar stich raveled   *travelled*
and unraveled each night, to slowly   *only*
weave the hours—a tapestry going nowhere,   *air:*
except perhaps to inch towards   *words.*
impertinence, a kind of quiet   *Yet,*
resistance. My triumph is failing   *ailing,*
to complete anything. Why   *I*
do I keep weaving this history   *story*
when in the dark each night I must   *us*
undo it all again? Telling and   *an*
retelling might keep us unending.   *ending.*

LITANY AT NIGHTTIDE

I am weaving the flung strands back together,
    after the night predictably unravels them.

A palimpsest—in which I find the buried fibers:
    the first time your eyes caught my laugh,

your incorrigible juggling,
    dropping a pear mask a stolen kiss,

the feigned somberness
    you wore around my father. Remember

how we first flared like lit conifers—
    struck flint finding its heat.

You were mischief, I was clever enough
    to catch–and keep.

I'd watch you plough the seedless ground,
    your shoulders blood-flushed in the sun,

a coolness in your grin;
    your words—not breathless at all.

We wed mind to mind, the instinct
    of our limbs not far behind. But when

you reappear—query of smoke
    vining around my arms—

will you have found the soul you sought—
    your own.

Before a hand writes over us, will you bring it to me,
    bare and shivering—

I will expose mine,
    toss it high to slice the dark.

Steer your ship towards it.

MY SON, AFTER YOU LEFT

without saying goodbye—
I understood why you asked advice

of everyone but me. Needing
to leave me was the point.

I cannot fault you for thinking
I would fall apart over our parting—

both wholly correct and not,
considering I have relinquished you

since the second you abandoned my body
to emptiness. Its waters evacuated

to the ocean, which you now rush toward.
Children always long for the sea,

never knowing how it suffocates
their mothers in the night.

(This is not to guilt you, but only
to explain what you cannot fathom

until you watch your own seed skip into some sea.)
No matter how we may so blessedly forget

the first terrors of inescapable labor,
cutting a body from our own,

even as you nuzzled, rolled up like a bun,
in the crook of your father's arm, my palm

encompassing your entire back,
even then, my womb groaned.

The body knows.
It is always letting go.

FRAGMENT: [HER RAGE AT THE GODS]

You desire faith from us

like flint catching the fire within wine

yet you inflict

we cannot see   except

disguised

gaze of disquieting stranger

those we love   vanish

like incense above the stoneface

remains   skeletal

salvage   body

news of return   flames

kneads   an ache

yeast punched down to rise

from dormancy   bruise

unbearable to wake

IN EXILE

Odysseus, witness
      over the starboard in the sea:
            lights of Ursa smashed upon the waves,

your face and shoulders
      mirrored in silver till they break—
            limbed in different pools.

I am exiled where I sit,
      a low tide abandoned by the waves:
            husband, son, the hollow

I have come to call myself,
      drifting. No wonder I fling out
            for some iron to anchor me—

Hands that peel mine open
      in the garden, let spill
            a crack of light,

like a torch thrown in a cave—
      a cruel exposure
            of its emptiness.

I know, as I know
      the freckles on my forearm
            you would trace, pillowed,

into the pattern of a bear,
      this hollow will never
            close—this longing

rivering down my limbs—
      like your hands shaping the beast—
            the loping constellation.

I cannot shed you.
　　　Wherever you are, I wear you
　　　　　on my skin.

QUOTIDIAN REBELLIONS

Why do I daily compose
these words as carefully
as I arrange the slip
of lace beneath my clothes?

Neither will be known.
As some pearlescent creature
beneath the sea slips unseen,
then suddenly—is lifted, blown

onto the lit shore,
for us suddenly to know
how much we do not know.
Sometimes at dawn we score

one of these bright entities
upon the beached foam.
For what has its beauty been?
And for whom? Hermes,

do you wander there? Apollo,
do you follow, ferrying
your light where no light goes?
Where shadows swallow

all. Or here: in the irrelevance
of a woman's dim closet,
or her darker, crowded dreams?
Here lies my act of rebellious

love: so softly to dress
the body, redress all unseen
thoughts, till each becomes known,
till the needs of each are addressed.

THE BEDROOM BUILT AROUND A TREE

My hands, with nothing else to touch, linger
    along the grains of our bedframe, as firm

and smooth to stroke as muscle cloaked in skin.
    Immovable. You carved it from a trunk of olive.

Its roots, like a constellation of stars,
    still stretch beneath it, gripping the ground,

as if we two were lifted by a net of light
    each night, lying above a burning meteor—

a relic of petrified, once-dripping sap.
    Dust motes also flicker amber in a crack

of light that beckons in the shape of you—
    which the curtains, drawn, quickly dispel.

Without you, I fear that I am making you
    more perfect in memory, and therefore, less.

Your constant humming, your heavy footfalls
    in the morning—how they irritated me.

Appear. Enrage me out of vapid apparitions.
    I want you as you. My chosen opposition.

LITANY AFTER READING BIRDFLIGHT

I have glimpsed my image in the glass of sea, like Narcissus.

I have turned away, preferring the velvet of cold sand inches beneath the surface.

I have imagined myself, bodiless, flying to you over the sea, returning to my skin after a long sleep.

I have lived every year, touching the green, veined and withering.

Here in the garden, I have seen myself more clearly: a woven art of bone and sinew, witnessed by countless sparrows.

I will not fly to you again, a thin chimera vanishing.

I will taste you in the flesh of this palmed, ripe peach.

AGRIOLOÚLOUDO

[Wildflowers]

Earth is embroidered with garlands of goldenrod draping the river's edge;

lavender hyacinth spicing the dawn with her fingertips drenched with scent;

roseate poppies that open like thighs of young lovers; and purple phlox

flush beneath limbs on the meadowlands; goblets of clover befuddling the

bees with their drunken and lilting dance—

                               Dazzle! Oh, amorous wildflowers—

flint us with fearlessness: yielding yourselves, every cell, to the radiance.

TESTAMENT: TO MY SON TELEMACHUS

My gift to you:
> *imperfect sight, the cradle of my voice,*
> *rivers of hair, my sea of bones,*

all bestowed on you—
> *a net lifted from my body*
> *to feed other streams.*

You will share yourself
> *the way fish give*
> *their bodies to the sea,*

my resolute and restless breaker:
> *work of my fingers relinquished,*
> *a chiseled shell singing.*

And I will be left
> *like Pygmalion's marble woman—*
> *carved by your need into something living,*

your gift to me.

LITANY AT LOW TIDE

When the seafoam heaps like beaten egg whites,

when shells gem the wet, indented sand,

when the cut gem on my hand sits heavier than a ghost,

when your hand at last slips like a picked shell into my hand,

we will find ourselves
        red-eared in disagreement.

We will argue
        away from children's ears.

We will turn away from the too-tense gaze
        of thirst

                to stir the sea kelp with a stick,

                to rinse our hands and lick the mineral beads
                        from each other's skin.

We will revel under the lit wicks
        of Leo chasing Orion from the sky;

the dunes—our shifting bed;

        each night rising
                into the marriage that we never had.

Interlude:

In Which Sirens Crying Beauty Will Lure You with Your Story

SONG OF THE SIRENS

In honeyed song, we do not mean to hurt you. Cursed
to bear the emerald mirror of the world, we voice
to passing souls our sole and shimmering view: the reverse
of the tapestry, through-line of each thread's purpose.

It's beauty—not ourselves—that beckons, stabbing through
your armor. The haze of days in which you're drifting—
dispelled—because you ache to know your life's true value,
its weight. The entire thread, unwound to its beginning.

Revere the mystery of living; it's an antidote
to us. You err in jumping ship just so you'll know
your glory, the point of all your gutting pain. Take note
of the broken bones, the skulls and sun-flayed skin below,

the overlooked and unvoiced message we are sending:
to hear your story, it must already have an ending.

Book IV:

Binding the Selvage

THE RETURN OF TELEMACHUS

This day, this blue brisk day,
made of wind and minutes—

minutes that filled
the fidgeting, wet days—

the wind scatters them
in a mere second,

like leaf litter illuminated
and blown away—

the ground now
clear for plowing.

Oh, bless this gale
that gathered and aimed you

home—my arrow—
to fly and pierce again.

TESTING ODYSSEUS

You have returned, disguised. I know it's you—
yet I stay silent. The spring bulbs rupture
and split the ground, but still stay firmly closed,
entombed during the sun's wearying circuit.

You are not the sun—let us be clear.
For here you are, yet the petals shut themselves.
In this trope, I am no lily—having weathered
too many winters above the shucked ground.

You're the vagabond who can be anywhere
but here. The marksman who can mark anything
but time. And you may be the flower, for once.
For you've returned, but still you are not open.

Mark this excessive distance, Odysseus.
Show me that your arrow can still fly home.

THE DUPLICITY OF WISDOM

A jester, who tells us: have an honest face
       but be cunning enough to mask it.

Like you, hidden within
       your hollow horse at the Trojan gate.

But see, the tale only gets told—
       the wit applauded—upon discovery:

bodies of men spilling like ants
       from the carved, equine belly,

or—my nightly trickery
       with the loom, unspooled.

It's true, we are truest when hidden.
       We are only knowable unveiled.

There lies the trick
       of the labyrinth of wisdom:

to know how to hide
       in plain sight;

to know the time
       to let yourself be known.

FOR THE SAKE OF TIME, SOME DETAILS WERE OMITTED

The monthly cleaning of sandal straps,
    kneading arches of worn feet each night,

how long it takes to dye
    and spin anything resembling thread,

each new phrase our son would mimic,
    all the times the gods didn't speak,

the slaughter of the wolf-pack of suitors
    on Apollo's feast day,

the strung bow's thwack
    after each arrow's release.

My relief at one man's absence,
    having sent him away—

the freedom a frail fidelity lavished on him.
    The feeling of a knife-twisted gut

at the smell of the hall
    sticky with entrails and incense,

the blood spreading
    like poppies in the wind.

The violence of return
    even apart from the violence.

How I feared you;
    how I wanted you. Eventually,

how you would tell me anything I asked;
    how I would tell you everything.

FRAGMENT: [YOU HOLD]

you hold my swollen discontent
like a pink liver slipped out of an incision

obscene the way it glints
in the light, drawing attention to itself

dislodged   shivering

a star   to plummet

until

Dawn, with her fingertips of hyssop

BATTENING THE SEA

What word
      could we inhabit,

cradle like a child's
      carved boat

into the silence—
      a sea between us?

What home can handle
      this inked deep?

The sea darkens beneath,
      wrinkles blue above.

We witness from this ship
      called marriage:

love, like a school
      of fish practicing

their precarious
      and fluid union.

THE BRIGHTNESS

I thought that you, and your return, would answer
       everything: all disappointment, expectation.

Unreal, of course. You would always prove
       both less than enough and far too much,

like a summer's day when the mist evaporates.
       The sun: first cloaked, then all at once abrasive,

overbearing. Our bodies—damp with sweat.
       How the sun bears its unimaginable heat

is all the more unclear for being visible.
       And I thought your absence was the mystery.

Set down your burning self and rest unseen awhile,
       my love. I'll rise in the evening, not a moon

to reflect you, but as the night jasmine opens:
       always in the dark with its own brightness.

ODYSSEY

Some sailors have swapped the word
    journey with your name.

        As if this sums up
            the whole story:

                You voyaged. I waited. As if
                    the unknown is only monsters

                    and a cliffed horizon.
                        And the keenest exploration is not

                the hazardous waters between
                    the mind and jagged heart.

          I have mapped that passage
              with many crossings, my love,

      clear enough for you
          to sail it in my wake.

IN THE DARK

you speak of a blind poet
who told your story, not knowing

he sang before its hero,
and how you held his air

like a shell pressed to your ear—
a found pearl cupped in a palm of sea

fearful of it slipping.
You tell me that you wept in company.

You, the lion's share of laughter,
a shiver—whispering

that the hairs of your beard
brimmed with tears

to water those you left behind—
like barren bulbs bleached in the dust.

A rinsed cup: you were filled
with ardor for the singer, king,

and strangers of that warm shore—
a sun-burnt foreigner too often, even to yourself.

Now you lie quiet—cool vein of quartz—
while I dream of dark brows

I never knew, including this distant you.
My fingers seek your face,

tracing each ridged scar and line—
the arched passage of your cheek—

like a blind man learning someone's shape
so he can sing what no one else can see.

WEEPING PENELOPE

Your old nurse maid took to calling me
      and it stuck
           like a sob in the throat.

I'm not saying it isn't accurate—
      I have sopped up sorrow like a sponge.
        Still, what bursts back:

our son's cackles from the kitchen,
      a starling trilling in the pregnant pear tree,
        the juices spilling down our wrists—

all those years of waiting,
      and what I remember
        most is joy—

a garment we put on with you gone—
      feigning cheer—and in this theatre,
        finding something deeper.

AN OFFERING WITH THE DAWN

In my clinging
discontent, come

and rinse me
like a hard and sudden rain.

Remind me of the sun
singeing us on the grass

in Athens. The lithe forms
of gods and heroines

looking as slack-limbed of love as us—
yet marble-hearted.

Laugh, my love, and let us
relinquish their bliss.

To you, I offer this:
myself, pierceable and living.

APOLOGIES TO EROS

Too often, I mistook you
      for a twisted hankering:
            a prankster making

our passions your playthings.
      Too often, I failed to notice
            how longing pours on all of us, how

rain caresses roots
      that snake into the dark
            far deeper than the oak's crown rises

to its zenith; and how
      those never-slaking,
            ache-inducing drops

could still call something
      green and buried in me
            back to its spring.

HEMEROCALLIS

[Daylily]

To say, I have been beautiful for a day—
To say, Now it is dark—

To say, I have been beautiful
     now it is dark—

To let darkness
     sheathe this moment
          before it fades—

     the way we cup the daylilies:
          petals, ruffled; stamen, saffron;

     gently snapping each short stem
          to make a bed of them beside our bed,

     breathing the scent of one spent day,
          rumpled by the night.

To be as ready to close
     having opened,
          many-petalled luster,
             to the sun.

And to say, What are years of waiting
     when we can turn from anything?

And to say, Enough—
And to say, A day—
     one has been enough.

ISLAND, SEA

This island, drenched with green, appears
nearly black in the dense morning—

the coming sun will drape it with color.
Birds rustle as I pass what's left of a ruin—

echoes in the packed loam, vacant
of the stones an old farmer reclaimed

to build a stairway to the sea: useful.
And beautiful to descend, to the million grains

of sand, and a blue too endless to excavate.
I climb down—a lone inhale—until

a whale's breath bursts the surface:
liquid grey luminesced for an instant.

I think of you. Still so much unexplained—
such curiosities emerging from your sea.

These many years, I've mastered
letting the waters be. Vast as you are,

you will not fill my valleys. Our love:
wholly incomplete. We will remain

to each a willful mystery; ourselves
autonomous and joined as island, sea.

Mary Romero's poems have appeared in *Birmingham Poetry Review, Crux, Measure, Able Muse, Mezzo Cammin, Peacock Journal, Christianity and Literature, Forma*, and *Blue Mountain Review*, among other journals. Her poetry has been nominated for Best of the Net, and her chapbook *Philoxenia* won the Luci Shaw prize. She currently lives in Chattanooga, Tennessee where she works as a deacon for the Mission Chattanooga, as well as a teacher, writer, and mother of two lovely hooligans. *Loom* is her first full-length collection. More of her work can be found at maryromero.net.

CPSIA information can be obtained
at www.ICGtesting.com
Printed in the USA
BVHW071352090522
636552BV00002B/148